Budgeting:
Your Personal Finance
Quick Start Guide

By

David Beich

COPYRIGHT

Dedicated to my loving parents and wife.

ACKNOWLEDGMENTS

I would like to thank my parents and wife for all their encouragement and coaching that have helped me discover many of the secrets found in this book.

CONTENTS

INTRODUCTION

Welcome! Why Budget? Understanding the Importance of Financial Management and Goal Setting.

Congratulations on taking the first step towards improving your financial well-being by picking up this book! In the fast-paced and ever-changing world we live in, managing money effectively has become an essential skill. Yet, many people find themselves struggling to keep their finances in order, leading to stress, anxiety, and the feeling of being overwhelmed.

In this chapter, we will explore the fundamental principles of budgeting and the reasons why it is crucial for achieving financial stability and success. We will delve into the power of goal setting, understanding how your financial aspirations can shape your budgeting journey.

1. The Importance of Financial Management

Financial management refers to the process of planning, organizing, directing, and controlling your financial resources to achieve specific goals. It is like steering a ship towards a chosen destination, with each decision and action contributing to the overall journey.

At its core, financial management involves making informed choices about how to allocate your income, control expenses, save, invest, and manage debt. By adopting effective financial management practices, you can gain better control over your money and work towards attaining your dreams, whether that's buying a home, retiring comfortably, funding your child's education, or pursuing your passions.

2. The Power of Budgeting

A budget serves as a roadmap for your financial journey. It is a tool that empowers you to make intentional and well-informed choices about your money. A well-crafted budget enables you to allocate your income wisely, ensuring that you cover your essential expenses while setting aside money for your goals and aspirations.

Think of a budget as a financial GPS - it guides you through life's financial complexities, helping you make course corrections when necessary and keeping you on track to reach your desired destination. Without a budget, it's like navigating through unfamiliar terrain without a map, leaving you vulnerable to overspending, debt accumulation, and a lack of progress towards your financial goals.

3. Benefits of Budgeting

1. **Financial Clarity**: A budget provides you with a clear picture of your income and expenses, allowing you to identify areas where you can save or cut back.

2. **Debt Management**: By budgeting and allocating funds to pay off debts strategically, you can free yourself from the burden of high-interest loans and credit card balances.

3. **Goal Achievement**: Budgeting enables you to set specific financial goals and allocate funds towards achieving them. Whether it's saving for a vacation, buying a car, or building an emergency fund, a budget helps turn dreams into reality.

4. **Reduced Financial Stress**: With a budget in place, you'll have greater control over your finances, leading to reduced stress and anxiety about money matters.

5. **Emergency Preparedness**: By budgeting for emergencies and setting up an emergency fund, you can weather unexpected financial storms without derailing your progress.

6. **Improved Relationships**: Budgeting can lead to healthier financial discussions and decisions within families or partnerships, fostering better relationships and shared financial goals.

4. Setting Financial Goals

While budgeting is a valuable tool for managing your day-to-day finances, it becomes even more powerful when aligned with clear financial goals. Goals provide the motivation and direction for your financial journey. They give you a sense of purpose and make budgeting more than just a series of numbers; it becomes a means to fulfill your aspirations.

When setting financial goals, it's essential to make them specific, measurable, achievable, relevant, and time-bound (SMART). For example, instead of stating, "I want to save more money," a SMART goal would be, "I will save $5,000 in the next 12 months to create an emergency fund."

5. Conclusion

In conclusion, budgeting is the cornerstone of sound financial management. It empowers you to take control of your money, plan for the future, and achieve your dreams. By setting clear financial goals and crafting a well-thought-out budget, you are taking significant steps towards financial freedom and security. In the following chapters, we will explore practical strategies and tools to help you succeed in your budgeting journey. So, let's get started and unlock the true potential of your finances!

Addressing Financial Stress and Mental Health: Navigating Financial Anxiety and Seeking Professional Support

Money plays a significant role in our lives, influencing our choices, opportunities, and overall well-being. While responsible financial management can bring a sense of security and accomplishment, financial challenges and uncertainties can lead to stress and anxiety. In this chapter, we will explore the impact of financial stress on mental health and discuss strategies for coping with financial anxiety. We will also emphasize the importance of seeking professional support when needed to navigate through difficult times.

1. The Impact of Financial Stress on Mental Health

Financial stress can be a pervasive and overwhelming burden, affecting every aspect of our lives. When faced with mounting debt, living paycheck to paycheck, or uncertainty about the future, individuals may experience various emotional and psychological challenges. Some common impacts of financial stress on mental health include:

1. **Anxiety and Depression**: Persistent financial worries can lead to feelings of anxiety and depression, affecting mood, sleep patterns, and overall mental well-being.

2. **Relationship Strain**: Financial stress can strain relationships with partners, family members, and friends, leading to conflicts and a sense of isolation.

3. **Impaired Decision Making**: When overwhelmed by financial stress, individuals may struggle to make clear and rational decisions, leading to potential long-term consequences.

4. **Physical Health Issues**: Chronic stress related to financial concerns can contribute to physical health problems, such as headaches, high blood pressure, and digestive issues.

5. **Performance at Work or School**: Financial stress can distract individuals from their professional or educational responsibilities, impacting their performance and productivity.

2. Coping with Financial Anxiety

1. **Acknowledge and Communicate**: Recognize and acknowledge your feelings of financial stress. Talking openly about your concerns with a trusted friend, family member, or partner can provide relief and emotional support.

2. **Practice Mindfulness**: Engaging in mindfulness practices, such as meditation or deep breathing exercises, can help reduce anxiety and promote a sense of calm.

3. **Focus on What You Can Control**: Concentrate on areas of your finances that you can control, such as creating a budget, cutting unnecessary expenses, and setting achievable financial goals.

4. **Seek Financial Education**: Knowledge is empowering. Educate yourself about personal finance, budgeting, and debt management. The more informed you are, the better equipped you'll be to make sound financial decisions.

5. **Avoid Comparisons**: It's easy to fall into the trap of comparing your financial situation to others. Remember that everyone's journey is unique, and comparing yourself to others can exacerbate feelings of inadequacy.

6. **Engage in Self-Care**: Take care of your physical and emotional well-being. Engaging in regular exercise, maintaining a balanced diet, and getting enough sleep can help reduce stress.

3. Seeking Professional Support

Despite our best efforts, financial stress can become overwhelming and unmanageable. In such situations, seeking professional support can be an essential step towards regaining control of your mental and financial well-being.

1. **Financial Counselors**: Certified financial counselors can provide guidance and strategies for managing debt, creating budgets, and improving financial literacy.

2. **Therapists and Counselors**: Mental health professionals can help you address the emotional toll of financial stress, develop coping mechanisms, and improve overall mental well-being.

3. **Support Groups**: Joining support groups or online communities focused on financial stress can provide a sense of camaraderie and understanding, allowing you to share experiences and learn from others.

4. **Employee Assistance Programs (EAP)**: If available, EAPs offered by employers can connect you with confidential

counseling and support services to address various life challenges, including financial stress.

Financial stress is a common and natural response to the challenges that life presents. However, it's essential to recognize the impact it can have on mental health and take proactive steps to cope with anxiety and seek support when needed. Remember that financial well-being is not just about numbers; it's also about taking care of yourself and your mental health. By addressing financial stress and seeking professional assistance, you can build resilience, overcome challenges, and pave the way for a brighter financial future. Remember, you are not alone on this journey, and there is support available to help you through difficult times.

CHAPTER 1:
GETTING STARTED WITH BUDGETING

Welcome to the first chapter of our Personal Finance Quick Start Guide! In this chapter, we will lay the foundation for your financial success by delving into the world of budgeting. Budgeting is a powerful tool that empowers you to take control of your finances, make informed decisions, and achieve your financial goals. Whether you're just starting your financial journey or looking to improve your existing budgeting skills, this chapter will equip you with the knowledge and tools needed to get started.

1. Understanding the Importance of Budgeting

At its core, a budget is a roadmap for your money. It is a detailed plan that outlines your income, expenses, savings, and investments, allowing you to allocate your financial resources effectively. Budgeting enables you to live within your means, avoid debt traps, and make deliberate choices about how you want to spend and save your money.

2. The Benefits of Budgeting

1. **Financial Clarity**: A budget provides a clear overview of your financial situation, giving you insight into where your money is coming from and where it is going. With this clarity, you can identify areas where you can cut back on expenses and find opportunities to save more.

2. **Goal Achievement**: Budgeting allows you to set specific financial goals and allocate funds towards achieving them. Whether you aim to build an emergency fund, pay off debt, or save for a dream vacation, a budget helps you track your progress and stay focused on your objectives.

3. **Control over Spending**: By following a budget, you regain control over your spending habits. You can identify unnecessary expenses, prioritize essential needs, and curb impulse spending, resulting in better financial decisions.

4. **Reduced Financial Stress**: Financial worries can be a significant source of stress. A well-structured budget can provide peace of mind, knowing that you have a plan in place to manage your finances effectively.

3. Creating Your Budget

1. **Gather Financial Information**: To get started, collect all the necessary financial information, including your income sources (salary, side hustles, etc.) and regular expenses (rent/mortgage, utilities, groceries, etc.).

2. **Categorize Your Expenses**: Divide your expenses into categories such as housing, transportation, food, utilities, entertainment, savings, and debt payments. This breakdown will help you understand where your money is going.

3. **Set Realistic Goals**: Define your financial goals and prioritize them based on their importance. Start with short-term goals, such as paying off a credit card, and then move on to long-term goals like saving for retirement.

4. **Allocate Your Income**: Allocate your income to cover your essential expenses first. Then, assign funds to savings and debt payments. Any remaining money can be budgeted for discretionary spending.

5. **Track and Adjust**: Regularly track your spending and compare it to your budget. This process will help you identify areas where you may be overspending or underestimating costs. Adjust your budget accordingly to stay on track.

Budgeting is the key to financial success and a secure future. By creating a budget tailored to your specific needs and goals, you take charge of your finances and gain the freedom to achieve your dreams. Remember, budgeting is not about restriction; it's about making intentional choices that align with your values and aspirations.

In the next chapter, we will explore how to thrive at budgeting by emphasizing consistency and adaptability, ensuring you develop a strong foundation for your financial journey. So, let's dive in and unlock the power of budgeting!

How to Thrive at Budgeting: Emphasizing Consistency and Adaptability

Budgeting is not a one-time task but an ongoing process that requires dedication and commitment. To thrive at budgeting, it is essential to develop two key qualities: consistency and adaptability. In this chapter, we will explore why these qualities are vital for successful budgeting and how they can help you navigate through various financial situations.

1. Emphasizing Consistency in Budgeting

Consistency is the backbone of any successful budgeting strategy. It involves developing a habit of regularly monitoring and updating your budget. By consistently following your budget, you build financial discipline, allowing you to make smarter financial choices and stay on track with your goals.

The benefits of consistency in budgeting include:

1. **Financial Awareness**: Consistently reviewing your budget helps you become more aware of your spending habits, income patterns, and financial priorities. This awareness enables you to make informed decisions and avoid impulsive purchases.

2. **Improved Self-Control**: As you stick to your budget, you build self-control over your finances. You become less susceptible to the allure of unnecessary expenses and focus on what truly matters to you.

3. **Building Emergency Funds**: Consistency in saving regularly allows you to build emergency funds to handle unexpected expenses without derailing your financial progress.

4. **Reaching Financial Goals**: Consistent budgeting ensures you allocate funds towards your financial goals systematically. Over time, this consistent effort moves you closer to achieving your aspirations.

2. Embracing Adaptability in Budgeting

While consistency is crucial, life is full of surprises, and financial situations can change unexpectedly. Embracing adaptability in budgeting means being prepared to adjust your budget when necessary to accommodate these changes. This flexibility is essential in ensuring your budget remains relevant and effective in different circumstances.

The benefits of adaptability in budgeting include:

1. **Handling Financial Challenges**: Life events such as job loss, medical emergencies, or unexpected expenses can impact your finances. An adaptable budget allows you to navigate these challenges without losing control.

2. **Seizing Opportunities**: Budget adaptability enables you to take advantage of financial opportunities that may arise. For example, you may receive a bonus or find a lucrative investment opportunity, and an adaptable budget allows you to make the most of it.

3. **Accommodating Changing Goals**: As your life evolves, your financial goals may also change. An adaptable budget allows you to reallocate funds to new priorities and adjust your strategies accordingly.

4. **Reducing Stress**: An adaptable budget reduces stress by providing you with the confidence that you can handle unexpected changes and continue making progress toward your financial goals.

3. Combining Consistency and Adaptability

Balancing consistency and adaptability may seem challenging, but they are not mutually exclusive. In fact, they complement each other to create a robust budgeting approach.

To combine consistency and adaptability effectively:

1. **Review and Reassess Regularly**: Consistently review your budget at regular intervals, such as monthly or quarterly. This helps you identify areas where you need to be more flexible and adapt to changing circumstances.

2. **Be Realistic**: While setting financial goals, be realistic about your income, expenses, and savings capabilities. This approach allows you to develop a budget that is achievable and adaptable.

3. **Create Contingency Plans**: Anticipate potential financial challenges and create contingency plans. Having backup strategies in place ensures you can handle unexpected events without losing sight of your financial objectives.

Thriving at budgeting requires a delicate balance between consistency and adaptability. Emphasizing consistency allows you to develop financial discipline, while embracing adaptability ensures your budget remains effective in the face of change.

By combining these qualities, you can confidently navigate through various financial situations, seize opportunities, and make steady progress toward your dreams. In the following chapters, we will explore the practical tools and techniques that can support your journey to financial success. So, let's stay consistent, be adaptable, and unlock the full potential of our budgeting efforts!

Setting Financial Goals: Defining Short-term and Long-term Objectives for Financial Success

Imagine having a clear vision of your financial future – a roadmap that leads to achieving your dreams and aspirations. This is the power of setting financial goals. In this chapter, we will explore the art of goal setting and its crucial role in shaping your financial journey.

By defining both short-term and long-term objectives, you can build a solid foundation for financial success and create a path towards a more secure and fulfilling future.

1. The Importance of Financial Goals

Financial goals are the destination points in your financial journey. They give purpose and direction to your budgeting efforts, transforming them from mere numbers to meaningful objectives. Setting financial goals is essential for several reasons:

1. **Motivation**: Having clear financial goals provides motivation to stay committed to your budget and financial plan. They remind you why you are making certain financial choices and keep you focused on the bigger picture.

2. **Focus**: Financial goals help you prioritize your spending and saving. They guide you in making informed decisions about where to allocate your resources and what expenses to avoid.

3. **Measuring Progress**: Goals act as benchmarks to measure your financial progress. Regularly tracking your journey towards achieving these goals allows you to celebrate milestones and make adjustments as needed.

4. **Financial Resilience**: By setting specific goals, you create a safety net for unexpected financial challenges. Having a solid financial plan helps you weather storms and remain resilient during difficult times.

2. Defining Short-term Financial Goals

Short-term financial goals are objectives that you aim to achieve within a relatively short period, usually within the next six months to two years. These goals are essential stepping stones in your financial journey and may include:

1. **Building an Emergency Fund**: Setting aside funds to cover three to six months' worth of living expenses in case of unexpected events such as medical emergencies or job loss.

2. **Paying Off Debt**: Prioritizing the repayment of high-interest debts, such as credit cards or personal loans, to reduce financial stress and free up more funds for saving and investing.

3. **Creating a Budget**: Crafting a well-defined budget that aligns with your income, expenses, and financial priorities. A budget provides the structure needed to achieve all your financial goals effectively.

3. Defining Long-term Financial Goals

Long-term financial goals are aspirations that extend beyond two years and often span several decades. These goals have a more profound impact on your financial future and may include:

1. **Retirement Planning**: Accumulating enough savings to maintain a comfortable lifestyle during retirement. Contributing regularly to retirement accounts, such as a 401(k) or IRA, is vital for long-term financial security.

2. **Purchasing a Home**: Saving for a down payment on a home or paying off an existing mortgage to achieve homeownership.

3. **Education Fund**: Establishing a fund to support your or your children's education expenses, such as college tuition.

4. **Investing for Wealth Building**: Engaging in long-term investing to build wealth and generate passive income over time.

Setting financial goals is the cornerstone of a successful financial plan. Whether short-term or long-term, these objectives give purpose and direction to your financial decisions, driving you towards financial success. By defining clear goals, you gain motivation, focus, and resilience in managing your finances. Remember, financial goals are not set in stone; they can evolve as your life circumstances change. Regularly reviewing and updating your goals will ensure they remain relevant and reflective of your aspirations. In the next chapter, we will explore practical strategies for creating and maintaining a budget, allowing you to align your finances with your goals effectively. So, let's set our sights on the future and embark on the path to financial achievement!

Understanding Needs vs. Wants: Prioritizing Essential Expenses and Mindful Spending

In today's consumer-driven society, it's easy to fall into the trap of mistaking wants for needs. However, mastering the distinction between the two is a critical skill for successful budgeting and financial well-being. In this chapter, we will explore the concept of needs versus wants, how to differentiate them, and the importance of practicing mindful spending. By prioritizing essential expenses and being intentional with our financial choices, we can achieve a balanced and financially secure life.

1. Distinguishing Needs from Wants

Needs are the fundamental requirements for living a healthy and sustainable life. They are essential for survival and well-being, encompassing the necessities we cannot do without. Common examples of needs include:

1. **Food and Water**: A basic necessity for nourishment and survival.

2. **Shelter**: A safe and comfortable place to live, protecting us from the elements.

3. **Clothing**: Appropriate clothing to keep us warm and protected.

4. **Healthcare**: Access to medical care and essential health services.

Wants, on the other hand, are desires or preferences that enhance our quality of life but are not necessary for survival. Examples of wants include:

1. **Entertainment**: Non-essential activities like going to the movies or eating out.

2. **Travel and Vacations**: Experiencing new destinations and leisure activities.

3. **Gadgets and Luxury Items**: Non-essential electronic devices or high-end products.

2. The Importance of Prioritizing Needs

Understanding the difference between needs and wants allows us to prioritize essential expenses and ensure that our basic requirements are met before indulging in discretionary spending. By addressing needs first, we create a strong financial foundation that supports our overall well-being and financial security.

3. Practicing Mindful Spending

Mindful spending involves making intentional and conscious choices about how we use our money. By adopting mindful spending habits, we can avoid impulsive purchases and direct our resources towards what truly aligns with our values and goals.

Tips for Mindful Spending:

1. **Create a Budget**: A budget helps you allocate funds to your needs, wants, and financial goals. It serves as a guide for making mindful financial decisions.

2. **Pause Before Purchasing**: Before making a purchase, take a moment to evaluate whether it fulfills a genuine need or is simply a fleeting want.

3. **Assess Value and Utility**: Consider the long-term value and utility of the item or experience you wish to spend money on. Will it bring lasting satisfaction, or is it a momentary pleasure?

4. **Avoid Impulse Buying**: Give yourself time to think before making impulsive purchases. Delaying a non-essential purchase can help you determine if it's truly worth the cost.

5. **Practice Gratitude**: Be grateful for what you already have. Focusing on gratitude can reduce the desire for unnecessary purchases driven by comparison or materialism.

Understanding the distinction between needs and wants is crucial for maintaining a balanced and financially healthy life. By prioritizing essential expenses and practicing mindful spending, we can make intentional financial choices that align with our values and long-term goals. When we focus on fulfilling our needs first, we build a strong foundation for financial security and have the freedom to indulge in wants without compromising our financial well-being. In the following chapters, we will explore more strategies for effective budgeting and financial success. So, let's cultivate mindful spending habits and make the most of our financial resources for a fulfilling and prosperous life!

CHAPTER 2:
CREATING AND MAINTAINING A BUDGET

What is a Budget and How to Use Tools to Maintain One

A budget is the financial roadmap that guides you towards achieving your financial goals. It is a plan that outlines your income, expenses, and savings in a structured manner. Budgeting empowers you to take control of your money, make informed financial decisions, and build a solid foundation for a secure future. In this chapter, we will explore the concept of budgeting and the various tools available to help you create and maintain an effective budget.

1. What is a Budget?

At its core, a budget is a detailed breakdown of your financial inflows and outflows. It tracks your sources of income and categorizes your expenses, providing a clear overview of how your money is being utilized. A well-crafted budget helps you:

1. **Plan for the Future**: By allocating funds to specific categories, such as savings or investments, a budget allows you to plan for future financial goals.
2. **Control Spending**: A budget highlights areas of overspending and allows you to rein in unnecessary expenses.
3. **Identify Saving Opportunities**: Budgeting reveals opportunities to save more by allocating funds towards essential financial objectives.
4. **Build Financial Awareness**: Creating a budget enhances your understanding of your financial situation, fostering better money management habits.

2. Using Tools to Maintain a Budget

1. **Spreadsheets to Stay Organized & Plan into the Future**: Spreadsheets are versatile tools that allow you to create a customized budget tailored to your specific needs. You can use software like Microsoft Excel or Google Sheets to organize your income, expenses, and savings.

- o Budget Planner / Forecaster: Use this sheet to visualize your monthly income and allocate funds for various expenses and savings goals.
- o Vacation Expense Planner: Plan and set aside money for upcoming vacations or trips.
- o Debt Snowball Setup: Track and manage debt payments to accelerate debt elimination.
- o Subscriptions & Utilities Tracker: Keep a record of recurring expenses like subscription services and utility bills.
- o Bonuses Spreadsheet Ideas (Optional):
  - Net Worth Tracker: Monitor your net worth over time, including assets and liabilities.
  - Retirement Investments Tracker & Forecaster: Project your retirement savings and investments.
  - Dynamic Mortgage Amortization Table: Understand your mortgage payment schedule and plan for early payoff.
  - Loan Tracker: Monitor loan payments and outstanding balances.
  - Vehicle Loan Payment Tracker: Track car loan payments and progress towards ownership.
  - Family Cell Phone Expense Tracker: Manage cell phone expenses for the whole family.

3. Budgeting Monthly with an App:

Various user-friendly budgeting apps are available to simplify the budgeting process. These apps allow you to track expenses, set financial goals, and monitor your progress in real-time.

- EveryDollar: A popular app that follows a zero-based budgeting approach, where every dollar is assigned a specific purpose.
- Mint: Tracks your spending, sets budget categories, and sends alerts for overspending.
- PocketGuard: Provides an overview of your finances, helping you stay on top of your bills and financial goals.

4. Cash Envelopes or Separate Savings Account:

If you prefer a more tangible approach, cash envelopes are an effective method for budgeting. Allocate cash to specific envelopes for different spending categories, and once an envelope is empty, you stop spending in that category. Alternatively, open separate savings accounts for specific goals, such as an emergency fund or vacation fund.

Budgeting is a powerful tool for financial management, providing clarity and control over your money. Whether you choose spreadsheets or budgeting apps, the key is to find a method that suits your preferences and lifestyle. By using these tools to maintain your budget, you can confidently manage your finances, achieve your financial goals, and work towards a more prosperous future. In the upcoming chapters, we will explore strategies for sticking to a budget, saving more, and eliminating bad spending habits. So, let's get started and unlock the full potential of budgeting for financial success!

Budgeting with Spreadsheets: Organizing and Planning for Future Expenses

Budgeting with spreadsheets is a practical and effective way to gain control over your finances, allowing you to organize and plan for future expenses systematically. Spreadsheets offer flexibility and customization, making them suitable for individuals with varying financial needs and goals. With the ability to create personalized budget templates, you can tailor your spreadsheet to align with your unique financial situation, whether you're managing monthly expenses, saving for a dream vacation, or paying off debts.

One of the key advantages of using spreadsheets for budgeting is the ability to create comprehensive trackers for various financial aspects. By having separate sheets or tabs for each expense category, such as housing, utilities, transportation, and entertainment, you can analyze your spending patterns and identify areas for potential cost-cutting. Additionally, you can forecast future expenses, allowing you to prepare for major upcoming costs like vacations or home improvements.

Another valuable feature of budgeting with spreadsheets is the option to set up dynamic formulas and calculations. By linking different cells and ranges, you can automate calculations for income, expenses, savings, and even investment growth.

This automation reduces the need for manual data entry and saves time, while also providing accurate and up-to-date financial information.

Furthermore, budgeting with spreadsheets encourages regular financial tracking and accountability. By updating your spreadsheet regularly, you gain a clear overview of your financial progress over time. This increased awareness fosters a sense of responsibility and discipline, as you become more conscious of your spending habits and financial decisions.

Whether you prefer using Microsoft Excel, Google Sheets, or other spreadsheet software, the simple act of maintaining your budgeting spreadsheet empowers you to stay on top of your finances and make informed choices for a more secure and prosperous future.

Budget Planner / Forecaster: Visualizing Monthly Income and Expenses

A Budget Planner / Forecaster is a powerful tool that allows you to gain a comprehensive view of your monthly income and expenses, helping you make informed financial decisions and stay on track with your financial goals. This tool provides a structured layout where you can list all your income sources, such as salary, side hustles, or investment earnings, and categorize your expenses, including housing, utilities, transportation, groceries, entertainment, and more.

By visualizing your monthly income and expenses in a Budget Planner / Forecaster, you can easily determine whether your income covers all your essential needs and discretionary spending. This clarity helps you identify potential budgetary shortfalls and make necessary adjustments to achieve a balanced financial plan. Moreover, the planner helps you set financial goals by allocating funds to savings, debt repayment, and specific financial aspirations.

Using a Budget Planner / Forecaster also empowers you to project future financial scenarios. With the ability to input anticipated changes in income or expenses, you can forecast how your financial situation may evolve over time. This forecasting capability is particularly valuable when planning for significant life events, such as purchasing a home, starting a family, or retiring.

Additionally, a Budget Planner / Forecaster encourages accountability and discipline in managing your money. By regularly updating the planner with your actual income and expenses, you can monitor your financial progress and track how closely you adhere to your budget. This level of awareness enhances your financial decision-making, as you become more mindful of where your money is going and whether your spending aligns with your financial priorities.

In conclusion, a Budget Planner / Forecaster is an indispensable tool for achieving financial success. Its visual representation of monthly income and expenses provides clarity and insight, enabling you to allocate your resources effectively, plan for the future, and work towards your financial aspirations. By embracing this powerful budgeting tool, you take control of your finances, enhance your financial discipline, and set yourself on the path to a more secure and prosperous financial future.

Vacation Expense Planner: Saving for Memorable Getaways

The Vacation Expense Planner is a dedicated tool designed to help you save and budget for memorable getaways without derailing your overall financial plan. Taking a vacation is not only a well-deserved break from the daily routine but also an essential part of self-care and rejuvenation. By using this planner, you can allocate funds specifically for travel expenses, ensuring that your vacation doesn't become a financial burden.

With the Vacation Expense Planner, you can estimate the total cost of your dream vacation, including transportation, accommodation, food, activities, and any other anticipated expenses. By breaking down the overall cost into smaller, manageable categories, you can plan your savings more effectively and create a realistic timeline for your trip. This planner also serves as a motivational tool, allowing you to see your progress as you diligently save for your vacation over time.

The Vacation Expense Planner encourages you to be intentional and purposeful with your travel spending. Instead of relying on credit cards or dipping into your emergency fund, you can save in advance and enjoy your vacation worry-free. This approach ensures that you can fully embrace and savor every moment of your getaway without the stress of incurring debt. By using the Vacation Expense Planner, you can make your dream vacation a reality while maintaining a balanced and responsible approach to your finances.

Debt Snowball Setup: Paying off Debts Efficiently

The Debt Snowball Setup is a powerful debt repayment strategy that allows you to tackle your debts in a systematic and efficient manner, gaining momentum along the way. Inspired by the idea of starting small and building up, the debt snowball method helps you stay motivated and committed to becoming debt-free. This strategy is particularly effective for individuals with multiple debts, as it provides a clear and structured approach to eliminate them one by one.

To set up a debt snowball, first, list all your debts from smallest to largest, regardless of interest rates. The key is to focus on the debt with the smallest balance, as this will be your starting point. Continue making minimum payments on all your debts while allocating any extra funds you have towards paying off the smallest debt. By putting extra money towards the smallest balance, you can eliminate it more quickly, providing a sense of accomplishment and motivation.

As you pay off your smallest debt, the next step in the snowball setup is to direct the amount you were paying on the first debt towards the next smallest debt. This creates a "snowball effect," as the amount you can apply to the subsequent debts increases with each one paid off. This process continues until you have paid off all your debts, building momentum and confidence as you progress.

The Debt Snowball Setup is not only effective in terms of repayment efficiency but also psychologically rewarding. Celebrating the achievement of each debt eliminated reinforces your commitment to the debt repayment journey. This method taps into the human desire for visible progress and offers a clear path to financial freedom.

By using the Debt Snowball Setup, you can take charge of your financial situation, gain control over your debts, and pave the way for a debt-free future. As you continue with the debt snowball strategy, you'll witness your debts shrinking one by one, ultimately leading to a sense of empowerment and a strong foundation for improved financial health. So, let's begin your debt-free journey with the Debt Snowball Setup and work towards a more secure and debt-free future.

Subscriptions & Utilities Tracker: Keeping Monthly Costs in Check

In the modern age of digital services and convenience, it's easy to accumulate various subscriptions and utility expenses that can quickly add up and strain your budget. The Subscriptions & Utilities Tracker is a valuable tool that helps you stay on top of these recurring costs, ensuring you remain mindful of your spending and maintain financial control.

With the Subscriptions & Utilities Tracker, you can compile a comprehensive list of all your subscriptions, including streaming services, software subscriptions, gym memberships, and more. Additionally, it allows you to record your utility bills, such as electricity, water, internet, and phone bills. By having a centralized tracker, you can monitor the total costs of these expenses and assess whether they align with your budget and financial goals.

The tracker acts as a constant reminder to review your subscriptions and utilities regularly. It prompts you to evaluate whether you are getting value from each service or if there are any redundant or underutilized subscriptions. This assessment empowers you to make informed decisions about whether to continue, modify, or cancel certain subscriptions to better align with your priorities and reduce unnecessary expenses.

By using the Subscriptions & Utilities Tracker, you can avoid the common pitfall of forgetting about subscription renewals or underestimating the impact of utilities on your budget. Staying vigilant and proactive in tracking these expenses ensures that you can promptly address any unexpected price increases or billing errors, preventing them from spiraling out of control.

In conclusion, the Subscriptions & Utilities Tracker is a valuable ally in maintaining your monthly costs and achieving financial balance. By diligently monitoring and evaluating your subscriptions and utility expenses, you can make intentional choices that align with your financial priorities and keep your budget in check. Empowered with this knowledge, you can navigate the world of subscriptions and utilities with confidence, leading to more efficient spending and improved financial well-being.

Bonus Spreadsheet Ideas for Financial Progress and Planning

In addition to the core budgeting tools, the Bonus Spreadsheet Ideas offer optional yet powerful resources to monitor and manage various aspects of your financial journey. These spreadsheets go beyond the day-to-day expenses and delve into long-term financial goals, providing a comprehensive view of your overall financial health. By incorporating these ideas into your financial toolkit, you can effectively track your progress, plan for the future, and manage specific financial obligations.

1. Net Worth Tracker: Monitoring Financial Progress Over Time The Net Worth Tracker is a fundamental tool for assessing your financial well-being. It provides a snapshot of your total assets and liabilities, giving you an overview of your net worth. Regularly updating this tracker allows you to monitor your financial progress over time and make adjustments as needed. As you reduce debts and increase assets, your net worth should show a positive trend, reflecting your improving financial health and increasing wealth.

2. Retirement Investments Tracker & Forecaster: Preparing for the Future Planning for retirement is essential to secure your financial future. The Retirement Investments Tracker & Forecaster enables you to monitor the performance of your retirement investments, such as 401(k)s, IRAs, and other retirement accounts. It forecasts the potential growth of your investments over time, giving you insights into whether you're on track to meet your retirement goals. By consistently contributing to your retirement accounts and monitoring their progress, you can make informed decisions to ensure a comfortable retirement.

3. Dynamic Mortgage Amortization Table: Managing Home Loan Repayments For homeowners, a Dynamic Mortgage Amortization Table is a valuable tool to manage their home loan repayments. This table breaks down each monthly mortgage payment, showing the distribution between principal and interest. Additionally, it reveals how making extra payments can help shorten the loan term and save on interest. By exploring different scenarios, you can find the most suitable repayment strategy that aligns with your financial goals.

4. Loan Tracker: Keeping Tabs on Loans and Progress The Loan Tracker is a comprehensive tool to manage various loans, such as personal loans or student loans. It helps you stay organized by listing all your loans, including balances, interest rates, and payment schedules. Tracking your loan progress enables you to

monitor your debt reduction journey and make informed decisions about accelerating debt repayment.

5. Vehicle Loan Payment Tracker: Tracking Car Loan Payments For those with car loans, the Vehicle Loan Payment Tracker is an essential tool to keep track of monthly payments and remaining balances. By staying up-to-date on your car loan, you can ensure timely payments and identify opportunities to pay off the loan faster, reducing interest costs.

6. Family Cell Phone Expense Tracker: Managing Mobile Expenses With multiple cell phone plans and family members, the Family Cell Phone Expense Tracker is valuable for managing mobile expenses efficiently. This tool helps you track monthly costs, identify usage patterns, and explore potential cost-saving measures, such as family plans or data optimization.

In conclusion, the Bonuses Spreadsheet Ideas provide optional yet valuable tools to enhance your financial planning and management. From monitoring your net worth to planning for retirement, managing mortgage payments, and tracking various loans and expenses, these spreadsheets enable a more holistic approach to your finances. By integrating these ideas into your financial toolkit, you can gain deeper insights into your financial progress, identify opportunities for improvement, and make informed decisions that lead to a more secure and prosperous future.

Budgeting Monthly with an App: Utilizing User-friendly Apps Like EveryDollar

In the digital age, managing finances has become more convenient and accessible through the use of user-friendly budgeting apps. One such popular app that has gained widespread recognition for its effectiveness is EveryDollar. Budgeting apps like EveryDollar provide a seamless way to create and maintain budgets, helping users stay on top of their finances effortlessly. In this section, we will explore the benefits of budgeting monthly with an app like EveryDollar and how it can streamline your financial management.

EveryDollar is designed with simplicity and ease of use in mind, making it an ideal choice for beginners and experienced budgeters alike. The app follows the principle of zero-based budgeting, where every dollar is assigned a specific purpose. Users can easily set up their budget by allocating funds to various categories such as housing, transportation, groceries, entertainment, and savings. The app's intuitive interface allows you to adjust your budget as needed and track your spending in real-time.

One of the key advantages of using EveryDollar is its ability to sync with your bank accounts, credit cards, and other financial institutions. This automatic transaction import feature saves you time on manual data entry, ensuring that your budget remains up-to-date with accurate financial information. By effortlessly categorizing transactions, you can see exactly where your money is going and identify areas where you may need to make adjustments to stay within your budget.

EveryDollar also provides valuable insights into your financial progress through visualizations and reports. The app generates charts and graphs to illustrate your spending patterns, making it easier to spot trends and areas for improvement. You can set financial goals within the app and track your progress towards achieving them, which can serve as a powerful motivator to stay disciplined and focused on your objectives.

Moreover, EveryDollar offers the convenience of accessing your budget on multiple devices, including smartphones, tablets, and computers. This flexibility allows you to stay connected to your budget no matter where you are, making it easier to stay accountable and avoid overspending.

In conclusion, budgeting monthly with an app like EveryDollar is an efficient and effective way to manage your finances. The user-friendly interface, automatic transaction import, and insightful reports simplify the budgeting process and provide valuable financial insights. By utilizing EveryDollar or other similar budgeting apps, you can take control of your finances, stay on track with your financial goals, and pave the way to a more secure and prosperous financial future.

Cash Envelopes or Separate Savings Account: Practical Strategies for Managing Spending

When it comes to managing spending and staying on budget, two practical and effective strategies are using cash envelopes and maintaining separate savings accounts. These methods offer tangible and organized approaches to ensure that your spending aligns with your financial goals, prevent overspending, and promote mindful money management.

Cash envelopes are a physical budgeting method that involves allocating cash for specific spending categories. Each envelope represents a different expense category, such as groceries, entertainment, dining out, or personal allowances. At the beginning of each budgeting period (e.g., monthly or bi-weekly), you withdraw the budgeted amount for each category and place the cash into its corresponding envelope. Throughout the period, you use the money in each envelope for its designated purpose.

Using cash envelopes provides several benefits. Firstly, it creates a tangible connection between your budget and your spending. Seeing physical cash diminish in each envelope as you spend reinforces the idea that money is finite and must be managed wisely. Secondly, cash envelopes help you develop greater awareness of your spending habits, as you become more conscious of how much money you have left for each category. This heightened awareness reduces the likelihood of impulsive and unnecessary purchases, allowing you to stay within your budgeted limits.

On the other hand, maintaining separate savings accounts is a digital approach to managing spending and savings. Instead of using physical cash, you open multiple savings accounts, each designated for a specific financial goal or expense category. For example, you may have separate savings accounts for emergencies, vacations, car repairs, or home improvements. With online banking, it's easy to transfer money between your main checking account and these designated savings accounts.

This method offers similar advantages to cash envelopes but with added convenience and flexibility. By allocating funds into different savings accounts, you can clearly visualize your progress towards specific financial goals. You can set up automatic transfers to these accounts, ensuring that you consistently save money for each purpose. Moreover, separate savings accounts provide a buffer between your spending money and long-term savings, reducing the temptation to dip into funds meant for important financial objectives.

Both cash envelopes and separate savings accounts offer practical solutions to managing spending and achieving financial goals. The choice between these strategies depends on your personal preferences, financial habits, and lifestyle. Some people may prefer the tactile experience of cash envelopes, while others may find the digital organization of separate savings accounts more suitable.

In conclusion, incorporating cash envelopes or maintaining separate savings accounts into your financial routine can significantly enhance your spending management. By using these practical strategies, you can ensure that your spending aligns with your financial priorities, reduce impulsive expenses, and work towards achieving your long-term financial goals with greater efficiency and discipline.

CHAPTER 3:
ELIMINATING BAD SPENDING HABITS

Understanding Your Spending: Identifying and Analyzing Money Habits

Understanding your spending habits is a crucial step in taking control of your finances and achieving financial well-being. It involves closely examining how you use your money, identifying patterns and trends, and gaining insights into your financial behavior. By understanding your spending, you can make informed decisions, implement positive changes, and align your financial choices with your long-term goals.

The first step in understanding your spending is to track your expenses diligently. Keep a record of every purchase, whether big or small, for a designated period, such as a month or two. You can use various methods for tracking, from old-fashioned pen and paper to modern budgeting apps or spreadsheets. Tracking your expenses allows you to see where your money is going and provides a clear picture of your spending patterns.

Once you have a comprehensive list of your expenses, it's time to analyze the data. Categorize your expenses into groups such as housing, utilities, groceries, entertainment, transportation, and more. Analyzing these categories will help you identify which areas are essential and where you might be overspending. Look for any recurring or unnecessary expenses that you can cut back on to free up funds for savings or debt repayment.

Understanding your spending also involves reflecting on your financial decisions and the underlying emotions driving your purchases. Consider if certain expenses are motivated by impulse, stress, peer pressure, or societal expectations. Recognizing emotional spending patterns allows you to make mindful choices and prioritize what truly brings value and fulfillment to your life.

As you gain a deeper understanding of your spending habits, you may uncover areas for improvement. Set specific financial goals that align with your values and create a budget that reflects these objectives. Use the insights from your spending analysis to allocate funds to different categories based on their importance in achieving your goals.

Regularly reviewing and reassessing your spending habits is essential for maintaining financial health. As life circumstances change, your financial priorities may shift, necessitating adjustments to your budget. By consistently understanding your spending and making intentional financial choices, you can work towards a more secure and prosperous future.

In conclusion, understanding your spending is a foundational step in the journey towards financial success. By tracking and analyzing your expenses, you gain valuable insights into your financial behavior and can identify areas for improvement. Armed with this knowledge, you can make informed decisions, align your spending with your values and goals, and pave the way to a more mindful and fulfilling financial life. Remember, financial understanding is a continuous process, and by staying vigilant, you can build a solid foundation for a brighter financial future.

Tracking Expenses Weekly and Monthly: Staying Informed and In Control

Tracking expenses on a weekly and monthly basis is a powerful practice that allows you to stay informed about your spending patterns and maintain control over your finances. It offers a comprehensive view of your financial habits, enabling you to identify trends, make adjustments, and ensure that your spending aligns with your financial goals. In this section, we will explore the benefits of tracking expenses regularly and how it contributes to overall financial well-being.

Weekly tracking of expenses provides a more detailed and granular understanding of your day-to-day spending. By recording expenses on a weekly basis, you can capture smaller transactions that may go unnoticed in monthly overviews. This level of detail helps you identify potential areas of overspending and make timely adjustments to stay within your budget. Weekly tracking is particularly beneficial for individuals who prefer a more frequent and hands-on approach to managing their finances.

On the other hand, monthly tracking offers a broader perspective, giving you a comprehensive overview of your spending patterns over a longer period. By reviewing your expenses at the end of each month, you can assess how well you adhered to your budget and whether there were any unexpected or irregular expenses that need attention. Monthly tracking also enables you to observe any seasonal spending trends and plan ahead for future months.

Tracking expenses regularly, whether weekly or monthly, provides insights into your financial behavior and helps you make informed decisions. It allows you to see where your money is going, evaluate the effectiveness of your budget, and make adjustments as needed. For example, if you consistently overspend in a specific category, you can reallocate funds from other areas to compensate and maintain a balanced budget.

Furthermore, tracking expenses helps you stay accountable to your financial goals. It fosters a sense of responsibility and discipline, encouraging you to think twice before making impulsive purchases. The act of recording expenses also increases financial awareness, making you more mindful of your spending decisions and their long-term impact.

To track expenses effectively, you can use various methods, such as budgeting apps, spreadsheets, or simply pen and paper. Choose the approach that aligns with your preferences and lifestyle, ensuring that it is easy to maintain consistently.

In conclusion, tracking expenses on a weekly and monthly basis is a key aspect of effective financial management. It empowers you to stay informed about your spending habits, make informed decisions, and stay in control of your finances. By adopting this practice, you can identify areas for improvement, work towards your financial goals, and pave the way to a more secure and prosperous financial future. Remember, consistency is the key to success, so make tracking expenses a regular part of your financial routine.

CHAPTER 4:
PAYING OFF DEBT AND
BUILDING AN EMERGENCY FUND

Two essential pillars of financial stability and security are paying off debt and building an emergency fund. These financial practices provide a solid foundation for achieving long-term financial well-being and protecting yourself from unforeseen circumstances. In this section, we will explore the importance of paying off debt and creating an emergency fund, as well as practical steps to achieve these financial goals.

6. 1. Paying Off Debt:

Debt can be a significant burden on your financial journey, causing stress and hindering your ability to build wealth. Prioritizing debt repayment is crucial for several reasons:

a. Reducing Financial Stress: Carrying debt can lead to anxiety and stress, affecting your overall well-being. By working towards becoming debt-free, you can alleviate this emotional burden and gain peace of mind.

b. Saving on Interest: Interest on debt accumulates over time, increasing the overall cost of borrowing. Paying off debt promptly saves you money on interest and frees up funds for other financial goals.

c. Improving Credit Score: Reducing debt and making timely payments positively impacts your credit score, opening doors to better interest rates and financial opportunities in the future.

To pay off debt effectively, consider using the Debt Snowball Setup mentioned earlier. List your debts from smallest to largest and focus on eliminating one debt at a time while making minimum payments on the others. As you pay off each debt, roll the payment amount into the next one until all debts are cleared.

2. Building an Emergency Fund:

An emergency fund is a financial safety net that provides a buffer against unexpected expenses or emergencies. Having an emergency fund is essential for the following reasons:

a. Handling Unforeseen Events: Life is unpredictable, and emergencies such as medical expenses, car repairs, or sudden job loss can arise at any time. An emergency fund ensures that you can cover these expenses without resorting to high-interest debt or draining your savings.

b. Preventing Financial Setbacks: Without an emergency fund, unexpected costs can derail your financial progress and lead to debt accumulation. Having a safety net in place protects you from such setbacks.

c. Reducing Stress: Knowing that you have a financial cushion in case of emergencies brings peace of mind and reduces financial anxiety.

To build an emergency fund, start by setting aside a small portion of your income each month. Aim to save at least three to six months' worth of living expenses. Initially, this may seem like a daunting task, but with consistent contributions, your emergency fund will grow over time.

In conclusion, paying off debt and building an emergency fund are essential steps towards achieving financial stability and security. By eliminating debt, you free up resources to invest in your financial goals. Simultaneously, having an emergency fund provides peace of mind and protection against unexpected challenges.

As you work towards these financial objectives, remember that consistency, discipline, and a long-term perspective are key to success. By prioritizing debt repayment and emergency fund savings, you lay the groundwork for a brighter and more resilient financial future.

How to Attack Debt: The Debt Snowball Method and More

When facing multiple debts, it can be overwhelming and challenging to know where to start. However, with a strategic approach like the Debt Snowball Method and additional debt-attack strategies, you can take charge of your debt and work towards financial freedom. In this section, we will explore the Debt Snowball Method and other effective debt-attack strategies.

1. The Debt Snowball Method:

The Debt Snowball Method, popularized by financial expert Dave Ramsey, is a powerful and motivational strategy to pay off multiple debts systematically. The method involves the following steps:

a. List all your debts from smallest to largest balances, regardless of interest rates. b. Commit to making minimum payments on all debts. c. Allocate any extra funds or windfalls towards the smallest debt. d. Once the smallest debt is paid off, roll the payment amount into the next smallest debt. e. Repeat this process until all debts are paid off.

The Debt Snowball Method is effective because it prioritizes the psychological aspect of debt repayment. By starting with the smallest debt, you experience quick wins and a sense of accomplishment, which motivates you to tackle larger debts as you progress. This method builds momentum, just like a snowball rolling downhill, leading to increased confidence and discipline in your debt-attack journey.

2. The Debt Avalanche Method:

While the Debt Snowball Method focuses on paying off the smallest debts first, the Debt Avalanche Method prioritizes debts based on interest rates. With this approach, you list your debts from highest to lowest interest rates and allocate any extra funds towards the debt with the highest interest rate. Once the highest-interest debt is paid off, you move on to the next one with the second-highest interest rate, and so on.

The Debt Avalanche Method can save you more money on interest payments compared to the Debt Snowball Method, making it a more cost-efficient strategy. However, it may take longer to experience a sense of accomplishment because larger debts with higher interest rates may take longer to pay off.

3. Debt Consolidation:

Debt consolidation involves combining multiple debts into a single loan with a lower interest rate. This method simplifies debt repayment, as you only have to make one monthly payment instead of several. Debt consolidation can be achieved through personal loans, balance transfer credit cards, or home equity loans, among other options. While it streamlines repayment, it's essential to be disciplined and avoid accumulating new debts during this process.

4. Debt Negotiation:

For individuals facing overwhelming debt, debt negotiation or debt settlement can be an option. This involves negotiating with creditors to settle the debt for less than the full amount owed. Debt negotiation may have adverse effects on your credit score and should only be pursued when other debt-attack strategies are not feasible.

In conclusion, attacking debt is a crucial step towards achieving financial freedom and stability. Whether you choose the Debt Snowball Method, Debt Avalanche Method, or other debt-attack strategies, the key is to be consistent and disciplined in your approach.

By making a plan, staying focused on your financial goals, and actively working towards becoming debt-free, you take control of your financial future and pave the way to a more secure and prosperous life. Remember, every step you take towards paying off debt brings you closer to financial peace and the freedom to pursue your dreams.

Roll Over Unspent Money to Save for Bigger Expenses.

Rolling over unspent money to save for bigger expenses is a smart and effective strategy to achieve financial goals and build a strong financial foundation. Instead of spending every dollar as it comes in, this approach involves carrying over unspent funds from one budgeting period to the next. By doing so, you accumulate savings over time that can be allocated towards more significant expenses, planned purchases, or emergency needs.

The practice of rolling over unspent money encourages responsible spending habits and prevents wastefulness. It fosters a mindset of thoughtful budgeting, where you consciously assess each purchase and determine its alignment with your financial priorities. When you exercise restraint and avoid unnecessary spending, you free up funds to allocate towards future goals, such as an emergency fund, a vacation, or a major household purchase.

Moreover, rolling over unspent money provides financial flexibility and resilience. It allows you to be prepared for unexpected expenses without derailing your overall financial plan. By maintaining a surplus in your budget, you create a buffer against unforeseen events, reducing the need to rely on credit cards or loans to cover emergencies. This approach contributes to long-term financial stability and empowers you to confidently navigate life's financial challenges. Ultimately, rolling over unspent money is a powerful way to take control of your finances, prioritize your goals, and build a brighter financial future.

Building an Emergency Fund: Preparing for Unexpected Financial Challenges

An emergency fund is a critical component of financial planning that provides a safety net during times of unexpected financial challenges. Life is full of uncertainties, and having an emergency fund can make all the difference between financial stability and financial distress. In this section, we will explore the importance of building an emergency fund and how it can safeguard your financial well-being.

1. The Significance of an Emergency Fund:

An emergency fund is a pool of money set aside specifically to cover unexpected expenses or emergencies. It acts as a financial cushion, protecting you from the impact of unforeseen events such as medical emergencies, car repairs, job loss, or home repairs.

Without an emergency fund, individuals may be forced to rely on credit cards, loans, or other high-interest debt to manage unexpected expenses, leading to financial strain and potential long-term consequences.

2. Peace of Mind and Reduced Stress:

One of the primary benefits of having an emergency fund is the peace of mind it provides. Knowing that you have a financial safety net in place can alleviate stress and anxiety during times of crisis. Instead of worrying about how to cover unexpected expenses, you can focus on addressing the situation and finding solutions without the added burden of financial strain.

3. Avoiding Debt and Protecting Credit Score:

Having an emergency fund helps you avoid resorting to debt to handle emergencies. Borrowing money in times of crisis can lead to a debt cycle that becomes difficult to break free from. By having cash readily available in your emergency fund, you can pay for unexpected expenses outright and protect your credit score from potential damage caused by missed payments or high credit card balances.

4. Building Financial Resilience:

An emergency fund enhances your financial resilience by providing stability during challenging times. Whether it's a medical emergency, a sudden job loss, or an unexpected home repair, having an emergency fund ensures that you can continue to meet your financial obligations and weather the storm without sacrificing other financial goals.

How to Build an Emergency Fund:

Building an emergency fund requires discipline and consistency. Start by setting a realistic savings goal, such as three to six months' worth of living expenses, and create a timeline to achieve it. Set up automatic transfers to a separate savings account dedicated to your emergency fund, so you contribute regularly without having to think about it.

It's essential to view your emergency fund as a non-negotiable aspect of your financial plan. While it may take time to build a fully funded emergency fund, even having a partial fund in place can provide some level of protection.

In conclusion, building an emergency fund is an essential step towards financial security and peace of mind. By having cash reserves to handle unexpected financial challenges, you can protect yourself from the stress of living paycheck to paycheck and avoid falling into a cycle of debt. Having an emergency fund is a powerful demonstration of financial responsibility and provides you with the freedom to navigate life's uncertainties with confidence. So, prioritize building your emergency fund today, and rest assured that you are well-prepared to face whatever life throws your way.

CHAPTER 5:
BUDGETING BASED ON YOUR INCOME TYPE

Budgeting for Traditional/Static Income: Managing Consistent Paychecks

Budgeting with a traditional/static income involves managing consistent paychecks, which can provide a stable and predictable financial foundation. However, effective budgeting is still essential to make the most of your earnings, achieve financial goals, and maintain financial well-being. In this section, we will explore practical strategies for budgeting with traditional/static income and optimizing your financial management.

1. **Create a Comprehensive Budget:** Begin by creating a detailed budget that encompasses all essential expenses, discretionary spending, savings goals, and debt payments. Start with your after-tax income and allocate funds to each category based on priority and necessity. This budget acts as a roadmap for your finances, guiding your spending decisions and ensuring that you live within your means.

2. **Build an Emergency Fund:** Having a stable income allows you to establish an emergency fund more easily. Aim to save three to six months' worth of living expenses to provide a safety net in case of unexpected financial challenges. An emergency fund protects you from relying on credit or loans during difficult times and ensures you stay on track with your financial plan.

3. **Automate Savings and Bill Payments:** Take advantage of your consistent paychecks by automating savings contributions and bill payments. Set up automatic transfers to savings accounts and automatic bill payments to ensure you never miss a due date.

Automating these processes fosters financial discipline and avoids the temptation to spend money earmarked for savings or bills.

5. **Plan for Financial Goals:** With steady income, you can plan for short-term and long-term financial goals more effectively. Whether it's paying off debt, saving for a down payment on a home, or investing for retirement, having a consistent income allows you to allocate funds towards your goals consistently.

6. **Review and Adjust Regularly:** Budgeting is not a one-time task; it requires regular review and adjustments. Keep track of your actual expenses and compare them to your budget regularly. Identify areas where you may be overspending or underestimating costs and make necessary changes to stay on track.

In conclusion, budgeting for traditional/static income provides an opportunity for stability and financial planning. By creating a comprehensive budget, building an emergency fund, automating savings, and consistently working towards financial goals, you can optimize your financial management and create a solid financial future.

Budgeting for Irregular/Changing Income: Handling Fluctuating Earnings

Budgeting with irregular or changing income can be challenging, as it requires adaptability and flexibility to manage fluctuating earnings effectively. Irregular income may come from sources such as freelancing, commission-based work, seasonal jobs, or self-employment. In this section, we will explore practical strategies for budgeting with irregular/changing income and how to navigate the unique challenges it presents.

1. **Establish a Bare-Bones Budget:** Start by creating a bare-bones budget that covers essential expenses such as housing, utilities, groceries, and minimum debt payments. This budget serves as a baseline to ensure you can meet your basic needs even during periods of low income. Identify non-essential expenses that can be cut back during lean months.

2. **Build a Variable Income Buffer:** To manage fluctuating earnings, create a buffer by setting aside a portion of your higher-income months to cover expenses during lower-income months. This variable income buffer acts as a safety net and helps you maintain financial stability during unpredictable times.

3. **Prioritize an Emergency Fund:** An emergency fund is even more critical for individuals with irregular income. Aim to save a larger emergency fund, covering six to twelve months' worth of living expenses. This fund provides a crucial safety net during periods of no or limited income.

4. **Use a Zero-Based Budgeting Approach:** Zero-based budgeting involves allocating every dollar of income to specific categories. This approach ensures that you account for all income, whether high or low, and allocate it efficiently to meet financial obligations and achieve goals.

5. **Embrace a Rolling Budget:** With irregular income, a traditional monthly budget may not be effective. Consider adopting a rolling budget, where you plan and budget for a set number of weeks ahead. As each week ends, reassess your income and expenses and plan for the next set of weeks.

7. **Diversify Income Streams:** Seek opportunities to diversify your income streams to reduce reliance on a single source of irregular income. This could include part-time work, side gigs, or passive income streams.

In conclusion, budgeting with irregular/changing income requires adaptability and careful planning. By creating a bare-bones budget, building a variable income buffer, prioritizing an emergency fund, and adopting flexible budgeting approaches, you can navigate the challenges of fluctuating earnings and achieve financial stability and success. Remember to stay proactive, regularly reassess your budget, and maintain a positive mindset in the face of income variability. With effective budgeting and financial management, you can overcome the challenges of irregular income and work towards a secure and prosperous financial future.

CHAPTER 6:
PLANNING MEALS AND
REDUCING GROCERY BILLS

In Chapter 6 of "Budgeting: Personal Finance Quick Start Guide," we dive into the art of meal planning and savvy grocery shopping to optimize your budget and reduce unnecessary expenses. Planning meals and reducing grocery bills are essential components of effective budgeting, as food expenses can significantly impact your overall financial health. This chapter equips readers with practical strategies to make informed choices when it comes to food spending, without compromising on taste, nutrition, or variety.

1. **The Benefits of Meal Planning:** Meal planning offers numerous advantages, including cost savings, reduced food waste, and time efficiency. By pre-determining your meals for the week, you can create a well-organized shopping list, helping you buy only what you need and avoid impulse purchases. Additionally, planning meals enables you to make healthier choices, as you can incorporate balanced and nutritious options into your diet.

2. **Choosing Budget-Friendly Ingredients:** In this chapter, we explore how to identify budget-friendly ingredients without sacrificing flavor or nutrition. By opting for seasonal produce, buying in bulk, and choosing cost-effective protein sources, you can significantly reduce your grocery bills while still enjoying delicious and satisfying meals.

3. **Utilizing Leftovers and Batch Cooking:** Making the most of leftovers and practicing batch cooking are excellent ways to stretch your food budget. By repurposing ingredients into new dishes or preparing larger quantities for future meals, you can save time, money, and effort in the kitchen.

4. **Smart Grocery Shopping Tips:** We delve into smart grocery shopping strategies that empower readers to be savvy consumers. From comparing prices, using coupons and loyalty cards, to avoiding shopping on an empty stomach, these tips ensure you get the best value for your money and avoid unnecessary expenses.

5. **The Convenience Trap:** The chapter also addresses the convenience trap and how it can lead to overspending on processed or pre-packaged foods. We offer alternatives to balance convenience and cost-effectiveness, enabling readers to make budget-friendly choices without compromising their health and well-being.

In conclusion, Chapter 6 emphasizes the importance of meal planning and reducing grocery bills in achieving financial success. By adopting practical strategies to plan meals efficiently, shop wisely, and make cost-effective choices, readers can take control of their food spending and allocate more funds towards achieving their financial goals. This chapter equips individuals with the tools they need to master the art of meal planning and make mindful choices at the grocery store, promoting a healthier and more financially secure lifestyle.

Meal Planning and Grocery Budgeting: Saving Money and Reducing Waste

Meal planning and grocery budgeting go hand in hand as powerful tools to save money, reduce food waste, and make mindful choices in managing your finances. In this section, we explore the synergy between meal planning and grocery budgeting and how these practices contribute to both financial well-being and environmental sustainability.

1. Meal Planning: Maximizing Value and Efficiency

Meal planning involves strategizing your meals for a designated period, typically a week, to ensure you have a well-thought-out menu and shopping list. By taking the time to plan your meals, you can maximize the value of every ingredient you buy and minimize the chances of buying items you don't need. This leads to significant cost savings and reduces the temptation to dine out or order takeout on impulse.

2. Reducing Food Waste: A Sustainable Approach

Food waste is a major global issue with significant financial and environmental implications. Meal planning plays a crucial role in reducing food waste by allowing you to use ingredients efficiently and creatively. By knowing exactly what you need and how much you'll use, you can avoid overbuying perishables that may go bad before you get a chance to use them.

3. Embracing Flexibility: Adapting to Sales and Seasonal Produce

While meal planning provides structure, it's essential to embrace flexibility and adapt to sales and seasonal produce. Keeping an eye on discounts, promotions, and seasonal fruits and vegetables allows you to capitalize on cost savings and incorporate fresh and nutritious ingredients into your meals.

4. The Power of Batch Cooking

Batch cooking is a valuable strategy to save both time and money. By preparing larger quantities of meals and freezing leftovers, you can stretch your grocery budget over several meals. This approach is not only economical but also convenient, as you have homemade, ready-to-eat meals available whenever you need them.

5. Setting a Realistic Grocery Budget

Having a grocery budget is a fundamental aspect of financial management. By setting a realistic budget for your grocery expenses, you gain control over your spending and can allocate funds efficiently between necessities, treats, and savings. Regularly tracking your grocery spending against your budget helps you stay accountable and make necessary adjustments as needed.

6. Embracing DIY and Smart Substitutions

Incorporating DIY practices and smart substitutions in your meal planning can significantly impact your grocery budget. From making your own sauces and dressings to replacing expensive ingredients with more affordable alternatives, these small changes add up to substantial savings over time.

In conclusion, meal planning and grocery budgeting form a dynamic duo that promotes financial prudence and sustainable living. By thoughtfully planning your meals, reducing food waste, and setting a realistic grocery budget, you can save money, improve your financial health, and minimize your ecological footprint. These practices not only benefit your wallet but also contribute to a healthier planet for future generations. Adopting meal planning and grocery budgeting as integral parts of your financial routine empowers you to make informed choices, nourish your body, and achieve financial well-being in harmony with the environment.

Using MealBoard App: Creating Efficient Weekly Meal Plans and Shopping Lists

In the digital age, technology has become an invaluable ally in managing various aspects of our lives, including personal finance and meal planning. Among the plethora of meal planning apps available, MealBoard stands out as a comprehensive and user-friendly tool that streamlines the process of creating efficient weekly meal plans and shopping lists.

In this section, we delve into the features and benefits of the MealBoard app and how it can revolutionize your meal planning and grocery shopping experience.

1. **All-in-One Meal Planning Solution:** MealBoard is more than just a recipe organizer or shopping list generator; it's an all-in-one meal planning solution. The app allows you to store recipes from various sources, including websites, cookbooks, and family favorites, all in one place. This convenience not only saves time

but also eliminates the need for multiple apps or physical recipe cards.

2. **Creating Customized Meal Plans:** With MealBoard, you can easily create customized meal plans for the week or even the month. The app offers flexibility in choosing recipes and assigning them to specific days, ensuring a well-balanced and varied menu. Whether you're following a specific diet, planning for special occasions, or accommodating family preferences, MealBoard adapts to your needs effortlessly.

3. **Efficient Shopping Lists:** One of the standout features of MealBoard is its ability to generate shopping lists based on your meal plans. As you select recipes for the week, the app automatically compiles the ingredients into a comprehensive shopping list. This intelligent feature eliminates the guesswork, prevents overbuying, and ensures you have everything you need for your meals.

4. **Budget-Friendly Ingredient Substitutions:** MealBoard goes the extra mile by suggesting budget-friendly ingredient substitutions for recipes. This feature helps you make smart choices at the grocery store and saves money without compromising on taste or nutrition. If a recipe calls for an expensive ingredient, the app will recommend more affordable alternatives, allowing you to stay within your grocery budget.

6. **Inventory Management:** Another valuable feature of MealBoard is its inventory management function. You can keep track of the ingredients you already have at home, which helps prevent food waste and unnecessary duplicate purchases. By incorporating items from your pantry and fridge into your meal planning, you optimize your grocery shopping and use what you have before it expires.

7. **Streamlined Grocery Shopping:** Using MealBoard's shopping list feature transforms your grocery shopping experience. The app

organizes the list by categories or aisles, making navigating the store a breeze. You can easily check off items as you shop, ensuring you don't miss anything and avoiding last-minute trips back to the store.

In conclusion, the MealBoard app is a game-changer for those seeking efficiency and organization in meal planning and grocery shopping. Its user-friendly interface, comprehensive features, and budget-conscious suggestions empower users to create efficient weekly meal plans and shopping lists. By leveraging technology, MealBoard simplifies the meal planning process, saves time and money, and contributes to more mindful and sustainable meal preparation. Whether you're a seasoned meal planner or new to the practice, MealBoard is a valuable companion that enhances your culinary journey and financial well-being.

CHAPTER 7:
PLANNING FOR LARGER EXPENSES AND FUTURE GOALS

Planning for larger expenses and future goals is an essential aspect of effective budgeting and financial management. Whether it's a major purchase, a home renovation project, funding education, or preparing for retirement, having a clear plan in place empowers you to achieve your aspirations and build a secure financial future. In this section, we explore the importance of planning for larger expenses and future goals, along with practical strategies to reach these milestones.

1. **Identifying Future Goals:** The first step in planning for larger expenses and future goals is to identify what you want to achieve. Take the time to envision your dreams and set specific, measurable, achievable, relevant, and time-bound (SMART) goals. Whether it's buying a home, starting a business, or saving for your children's education, having well-defined goals provides a clear direction for your financial planning.

2. **Creating a Separate Savings Fund:** Once you've set your goals, create separate savings funds or accounts for each objective. Having designated accounts allows you to track progress, avoid mingling funds, and maintain a clear focus on your goals. Automating regular contributions to these accounts ensures consistency and keeps you accountable to your savings targets.

3. **Establishing Timelines and Milestones:** Break down your larger expenses and future goals into smaller, achievable milestones. Setting timelines for each milestone creates a sense of urgency and helps you measure your progress. For example, if you're saving for a down payment on a house, you might set

quarterly savings targets to reach the required amount within a specific timeframe.

4. **Adjusting Your Budget:** Planning for larger expenses and future goals may require adjustments to your budget. Analyze your current spending habits and identify areas where you can cut back or reallocate funds towards your savings goals. Sacrificing small indulgences in the present can lead to significant rewards in the future.

5. **Considering Investment Opportunities:** Depending on your goals and timelines, consider investment opportunities to grow your savings. Consult with a financial advisor to explore investment options that align with your risk tolerance and financial objectives. Investments can help your money work harder for you and accelerate your progress towards achieving your goals.

6. **Revisiting and Revising Your Plan:** Life is dynamic, and circumstances may change over time. Regularly revisit and revise your plan as needed to account for changes in your financial situation or goals. Flexibility and adaptability are key to successful long-term financial planning.

In conclusion, planning for larger expenses and future goals is a fundamental pillar of financial success. By setting clear goals, creating separate savings funds, establishing timelines and milestones, adjusting your budget, considering investments, and staying adaptable, you pave the way for a financially secure and fulfilling future.

With disciplined and strategic planning, you can turn your dreams into reality and enjoy the satisfaction of achieving your most significant aspirations. Remember, planning is the key that unlocks the door to a brighter financial future, one step at a time.

Envelope Budgeting: Organizing Funds for Specific Purposes

Envelope budgeting is a simple yet powerful budgeting method that involves allocating cash into separate envelopes, each dedicated to a specific spending category. This traditional approach to budgeting is highly effective for individuals who prefer a tangible and visual way to manage their finances. In this section, we explore the concept of envelope budgeting, its benefits, and how to implement this method to take control of your spending and achieve your financial goals.

1. How Envelope Budgeting Works: With envelope budgeting, you divide your income into various envelopes, representing different spending categories such as groceries, utilities, entertainment, transportation, and more. Each envelope contains the exact amount of cash you have allocated for that specific category for the month. As you spend, you physically take money from the respective envelope, providing a clear visual of how much is left for that particular category.

2. Benefits of Envelope Budgeting: Envelope budgeting offers several advantages, particularly for those who prefer a tangible way of tracking their spending:

- **Financial Awareness:** Envelope budgeting promotes financial mindfulness as you are directly handling cash and becoming more conscious of your spending choices.

- **Control Over Spending:** When the envelope is empty, it signals that you have reached your spending limit for that category. This control helps prevent overspending and impulsive purchases.

- **Easy to Understand:** Envelope budgeting is straightforward and easy to understand, making it accessible to people of all financial literacy levels.

- **No Overdrafts or Credit Card Debt:** Since you are using cash, you are not at risk of overdrawing your account or accumulating credit card debt.

- **Adaptable to Irregular Incomes:** Envelope budgeting is particularly useful for individuals with irregular or changing incomes, as it allows them to allocate cash based on their earnings.

3. Implementing Envelope Budgeting: To get started with envelope budgeting, follow these steps:

- **Create Spending Categories:** Determine the main spending categories that align with your financial goals and lifestyle.

- **Allocate Funds:** Divide your income into the appropriate envelopes, ensuring you allocate enough for each category.

- **Use Cash:** Use cash for your day-to-day expenses, taking funds from the corresponding envelopes when necessary.

- **Replenish Envelopes:** At the beginning of each budgeting period (e.g., month or week), replenish the envelopes with the allocated funds.

- **Track and Adjust:** Keep a record of your spending and regularly assess your progress. Adjust the amounts in each envelope if needed to better align with your spending patterns.

4. Modern Envelope Budgeting Apps: While traditional envelope budgeting involves physical cash, several digital apps now replicate this method electronically. These apps allow you to create virtual envelopes and allocate funds to different categories. They provide the convenience of digital technology while preserving the principles of envelope budgeting.

In conclusion, envelope budgeting is a tried and true method that brings a sense of control and awareness to your financial life. By organizing funds for specific purposes, you gain clarity on your spending habits and can make more intentional choices. Whether you choose to use physical envelopes or modern envelope budgeting apps, this budgeting technique is a valuable tool to help you achieve your financial objectives and foster healthy financial habits for a brighter future.

Auto Debit into Extra Savings Account: Automated Savings for Goals and Projects

Automating your savings is a powerful strategy that can help you effortlessly reach your financial goals and projects. Setting up automatic transfers from your primary checking account into an extra savings account allows you to consistently save money without the need for manual intervention. In this section, we explore the concept of auto-debit into an extra savings account, its benefits, and how this automated approach can revolutionize your savings journey.

1. **The Power of Automation:** Automating your savings is a game-changer for individuals seeking to build a strong financial foundation. By setting up recurring transfers, you remove the burden of remembering to save each month. The process is seamless and occurs automatically, ensuring consistent progress towards your savings goals.

2. **Creating an Extra Savings Account:** To implement auto-debit savings, start by creating an extra savings account specifically dedicated to your goals and projects. This account acts as a separate space for your automated savings, preventing the funds from getting mixed up with your everyday expenses.

3. **Tailoring Savings for Different Goals:** Auto-debit savings allow you to allocate different amounts to various goals and projects. Whether you're saving for a down payment on a house, a dream vacation, emergency fund, or any other financial aspiration, you can set up multiple auto-debit transfers to address each objective separately.

4. **Consistency and Discipline:** Consistency is the key to successful savings. With auto-debit, you ensure that a portion of your income is set aside for savings before you have a chance to spend it elsewhere. This level of discipline strengthens your financial habits and helps you stay on track towards achieving your goals.

5. **Peace of Mind and Financial Security:** Automated savings provide peace of mind, knowing that you are actively working towards your financial goals. Whether it's building an emergency fund or saving for a future investment, having funds accumulate in your extra savings account offers financial security during uncertain times.

7. **Adaptability and Adjustability:** Auto-debit savings are adaptable to changes in your financial situation. If your income increases or decreases, you can easily adjust the automated transfers accordingly. This flexibility ensures that your savings plan remains aligned with your evolving circumstances.

8. **Leveraging Compound Interest:** By consistently contributing to your extra savings account, you harness the power of compound interest. Over time, your savings generate interest, and that interest, in turn, earns interest. This compounding effect accelerates your savings growth, helping you reach your goals faster.

In conclusion, auto-debit into an extra savings account is an excellent strategy for automating your savings and working towards your financial objectives. By leveraging the power of automation, you can cultivate consistent savings habits, achieve financial peace of mind, and unlock the potential of compound interest. Whether you're saving for short-term goals or long-term projects, automated savings provide the structure and discipline needed to build a solid financial future with ease and confidence. Embrace the convenience of auto-debit savings and take charge of your financial destiny today.

CHAPTER 8:
BASICS OF BUILDING WEALTH

In Chapter 8 of "Budgeting: Personal Finance Quick Start Guide," we explore the fundamental principles and strategies for building wealth and achieving long-term financial success. Building wealth is not about quick fixes or get-rich-quick schemes; it is a gradual and disciplined process that requires careful planning, prudent decision-making, and consistent efforts. This chapter lays the groundwork for individuals to cultivate a mindset and approach that will lead them towards a more prosperous future.

1. **Understanding the Concept of Wealth:** Wealth, in the context of personal finance, refers to the accumulation of assets and resources that surpass one's immediate needs. It involves having sufficient financial strength to cover expenses, save for future goals, and withstand unexpected challenges. Building wealth is about creating a solid financial foundation that allows you to enjoy financial freedom and security.

2. **Cultivating a Wealth-Building Mindset:** Building wealth begins with adopting a positive and proactive mindset. Believe in your ability to achieve your financial goals and embrace the mindset of a lifelong learner. Educate yourself about personal finance, stay informed about economic trends, and seek guidance from reputable financial resources.

3. **Managing Debt Wisely:** Debt management is a critical aspect of wealth-building. While certain debts, such as a mortgage or student loans, may be necessary, it is essential to manage them responsibly. Avoid accumulating high-interest debt, pay off outstanding balances, and create a plan to become debt-free over time.

4. **Emphasizing the Power of Saving:** Savings play a central role in building wealth. Consistently setting aside a portion of your income for savings allows you to build an emergency fund, achieve short-term goals, and invest for the future. Start with an achievable savings goal and gradually increase it as your financial situation improves.

5. **Investing for Long-Term Growth:** Investing is a crucial component of wealth-building, as it has the potential to generate long-term growth and outpace inflation. While this guide does not cover specific investment strategies that require a securities license, it emphasizes the importance of understanding your risk tolerance, diversification, and seeking professional advice when needed.

6. **Building Multiple Streams of Income:** Creating multiple streams of income can enhance your ability to build wealth. This may include diversifying your sources of income through side gigs, passive income ventures, or entrepreneurial pursuits. Multiple streams of income provide additional financial stability and the potential for increased savings and investments.

7. **Continuously Reevaluating Financial Goals:** As you progress on your wealth-building journey, regularly reevaluate your financial goals and adjust your strategies accordingly. Life circumstances change, and your financial objectives may evolve over time. Flexibility and adaptability are key to staying on track towards building wealth.

In conclusion, Chapter 8 lays the foundation for building wealth by promoting a proactive mindset, prudent debt management, consistent savings, and the importance of investing for the long term. Remember that building wealth is a gradual process, and success requires discipline, patience, and dedication. With a strong financial plan, a commitment to continuous learning, and sound decision-making, you can lay the groundwork for a financially prosperous future and achieve your long-term wealth-building goals.

CHAPTER 9:
INSURANCE COVERAGE AND LEGACY PLANNING

Importance of Insurance Coverage: Protecting Yourself and Your Assets

Insurance coverage plays a crucial role in safeguarding your financial well-being and providing peace of mind in the face of unforeseen events. Insurance serves as a safety net, protecting you and your assets from potential risks and losses that could have a significant impact on your financial stability. In this section, we explore the importance of insurance coverage and its role in providing financial protection.

1. **Risk Management:** Life is full of uncertainties, and unexpected events can happen at any time. Insurance serves as a risk management tool, helping you mitigate the financial impact of accidents, illnesses, natural disasters, and other unforeseen occurrences. Having appropriate insurance coverage ensures that you are prepared to handle these challenges without depleting your savings or going into debt.

2. **Protecting Your Loved Ones:** Insurance coverage not only safeguards your financial interests but also protects your loved ones in the event of your absence or disability. Life insurance, for example, provides financial support to your beneficiaries, ensuring that they can maintain their standard of living and fulfill their financial responsibilities.

3. **Safeguarding Your Assets:** Property and casualty insurance, such as homeowners and auto insurance, protects your assets from potential damage, theft, or liability. These coverages help

you avoid significant financial losses that could arise from accidents or incidents involving your property or vehicles.

4. **Ensuring Business Continuity:** For entrepreneurs and business owners, insurance is essential for ensuring business continuity and protection against unexpected liabilities or events that could disrupt operations. Business insurance can cover property damage, liability claims, and even provide coverage for key personnel.

5. **Complying with Legal Requirements:** In many cases, insurance coverage is legally required. For example, auto insurance is mandatory in most jurisdictions to protect drivers and others on the road. Additionally, if you have a mortgage on your home, your lender may require you to have homeowners insurance to protect their investment.

6. **Peace of Mind:** Knowing that you have insurance coverage in place provides peace of mind, allowing you to focus on other aspects of your life without constantly worrying about potential financial risks. With insurance, you can face life's uncertainties with confidence, knowing that you have a safety net to fall back on.

8. **Tailored Coverage to Your Needs:** Insurance is not a one-size-fits-all solution. Policies can be customized to meet your specific needs and risk profile. Working with a reputable insurance agent or broker can help you identify the right coverage for your unique circumstances.

In conclusion, insurance coverage is an essential component of financial planning, offering protection and security for you, your loved ones, and your assets. It serves as a valuable risk management tool, shielding you from financial losses and providing a safety net during challenging times. By ensuring that you have the appropriate insurance coverage tailored to your needs, you can rest assured that you are well-prepared to handle whatever life throws your way and maintain your financial well-being.

Legacy Planning: Preparing for the Future with Wills and Estate Planning

Legacy planning involves making thoughtful and intentional decisions about how you want your assets and belongings to be distributed after your passing. It goes beyond the distribution of wealth; it encompasses the preservation of your values, beliefs, and the impact you wish to leave on your loved ones and the causes you care about. In this section, we explore the importance of legacy planning, the key components involved, and the steps you can take to prepare for the future.

1. **Preserving Your Wishes:** Legacy planning ensures that your wishes are respected and carried out after your passing. By creating a comprehensive estate plan, you have the opportunity to designate beneficiaries, appoint guardians for minor children, and dictate how your assets should be distributed among family members and charitable causes.

2. **Minimizing Potential Conflicts:** Having a well-structured estate plan can minimize potential conflicts among family members and loved ones. Clear instructions and decisions in your will can reduce uncertainty and ambiguity, helping to avoid disputes and legal challenges regarding the distribution of your estate.

3. **Providing for Your Loved Ones:** One of the primary goals of legacy planning is to provide financial security for your loved ones after you're gone. Estate planning allows you to ensure that your assets and financial resources are distributed according to your wishes, providing for the well-being and future needs of your family members.

4. **Reducing Estate Taxes and Expenses:** Strategic estate planning can also help minimize estate taxes and administrative expenses. By exploring legal strategies and tax-saving options, you

can preserve a larger portion of your estate for your beneficiaries and charitable interests.

5. **Establishing Trusts and Philanthropic Giving:** Legacy planning often involves the establishment of trusts, which can protect and manage assets for the benefit of specific individuals or charitable organizations. Charitable giving through your estate plan allows you to support causes that are close to your heart, leaving a lasting impact on the community.

6. **Appointing Executors and Power of Attorney:** As part of your legacy planning, you can appoint trusted individuals as executors of your estate and grant power of attorney to handle financial and healthcare decisions on your behalf, should you become incapacitated.

7. **Regularly Reviewing and Updating Your Plan:** Life is dynamic, and circumstances can change over time. It is essential to regularly review and update your estate plan to reflect any changes in your family situation, financial status, or legal regulations.

In conclusion, legacy planning is a vital component of responsible financial management, allowing you to preserve your wishes, provide for your loved ones, and leave a positive impact on the world. Through thoughtful estate planning, you can ensure that your legacy continues beyond your lifetime, bringing peace of mind and clarity to you and your loved ones. By taking the necessary steps to plan for the future, you can rest assured that your hard-earned assets and values will be protected and celebrated for generations to come.

CHAPTER 10: CELEBRATING FINANCIAL MILESTONES

Acknowledging Success: Celebrating Achievements and Staying Motivated

In the journey of personal finance and budgeting, it's essential to celebrate achievements and milestones along the way. Acknowledging success not only boosts your motivation but also reinforces positive financial habits. In this section, we explore the importance of celebrating achievements, the impact it has on your financial journey, and practical ways to stay motivated on the path to financial success.

1. The Power of Recognition: Celebrating achievements, no matter how big or small, is a powerful tool for maintaining momentum in your financial journey. Recognizing your progress and successes reinforces the value of your efforts and encourages you to continue taking positive steps towards your financial goals.

2. Milestones as Stepping Stones: View financial milestones as stepping stones towards your larger objectives. Each milestone you achieve brings you closer to your ultimate financial destination, and celebrating these steps serves as a reminder of the progress you've made.

3. Boosting Motivation: Motivation is a key driver in any endeavor, and personal finance is no exception. By celebrating achievements, you inject a dose of positivity into your financial journey, rekindling your enthusiasm and dedication to stick to your budgeting and savings plans.

4. Reinforcing Positive Habits: Forming positive financial habits is essential for long-term success. By celebrating achievements, you reinforce these habits, making them more likely to become ingrained in your daily life. The act of celebrating success serves as positive reinforcement for the behaviors that contributed to your achievements.

5. Finding Balance: While celebrating achievements is crucial, it's equally important to strike a balance. Avoid extravagant celebrations that undermine the progress you've made or lead to overspending. Instead, opt for meaningful and budget-friendly ways to acknowledge your accomplishments.

6. Practical Ways to Celebrate: Celebrating financial achievements doesn't have to be extravagant or expensive. Consider these practical and budget-conscious ways to acknowledge your successes:

- **Reflect and Appreciate:** Take time to reflect on your achievements and the progress you've made. Acknowledge the hard work and dedication you've put into managing your finances.

- **Share with Loved Ones:** Celebrate with your loved ones who have supported you throughout your financial journey. Share your milestones and involve them in your celebration.

- **Set Rewards:** Establish small rewards for achieving specific financial goals. Treat yourself to a modest splurge, a favorite meal, or a relaxing day off.

- **Update Your Vision Board:** If you have a vision board or financial goals visualized, update it with new milestones you've reached. Seeing your achievements displayed visually can be a powerful motivator.

7. Setting New Challenges: Use celebrations as an opportunity to set new challenges and financial goals. Each achievement should fuel your ambition to take on bigger challenges and reach new heights in your financial journey.

In conclusion, acknowledging success and celebrating achievements are integral components of a successful financial journey. By recognizing your progress, staying motivated, and reinforcing positive habits, you can cultivate a mindset of growth and determination. Celebrating milestones, no matter how small, provides the inspiration needed to navigate the challenges of personal finance with confidence and optimism. Remember, your financial journey is about more than just numbers; it's about the journey itself and the accomplishments you achieve along the way. So, take a moment to celebrate your financial successes, and let that celebration fuel your determination to achieve even greater heights in your quest for financial well-being.

CONCLUSION

In "Budgeting: Your Personal Finance Quick Start Guide," we have delved into the essential principles and strategies to help you take control of your finances, achieve your financial goals, and build a secure and prosperous future. As we conclude this guide, let's recap the key budgeting strategies and financial tips that can empower you to navigate the world of personal finance with confidence and success.

1. **Embrace the Power of Budgeting:** Budgeting is the foundation of sound financial management. It provides a clear picture of your income and expenses, enabling you to make informed decisions, prioritize your spending, and allocate funds towards your goals.

2. **Consistency and Adaptability:** Consistency is key to successful budgeting. Regularly review your budget, track your expenses, and stay committed to your financial plan. Additionally, be adaptable and open to adjusting your budget as circumstances change.

3. **Set Clear Financial Goals:** Establish clear and achievable financial goals that align with your values and aspirations. Define short-term and long-term objectives, and use them as motivation to stay on track with your budgeting efforts.

4. **Prioritize Needs vs. Wants:** Distinguish between essential expenses and discretionary spending. Prioritize your needs over wants and make mindful spending choices to ensure your financial resources are directed towards what truly matters.

5. **Utilize Tools and Technology:** Leverage budgeting apps, spreadsheets, and digital tools to streamline your financial planning and tracking. These resources can help you stay organized, monitor progress, and make informed financial decisions.

6. **Manage Debt Strategically:** Address debt proactively by creating a debt repayment plan. Prioritize high-interest debts, explore consolidation options if necessary, and avoid accumulating new debt whenever possible.

8. **Save and Invest Wisely:** Cultivate a habit of saving consistently and prioritize building an emergency fund to handle unforeseen expenses. Additionally, explore investment opportunities that align with your risk tolerance and financial goals.

9. **Celebrate Achievements:** Acknowledge and celebrate your financial milestones and successes. Recognizing your achievements reinforces positive financial habits and motivates you to continue on your financial journey.

10. **Legacy Planning for the Future:** Consider the importance of legacy planning and estate management. Creating a comprehensive estate plan allows you to protect your loved ones and leave a lasting impact on the causes you care about.

11. **Seek Professional Guidance:** When needed, seek advice from reputable financial advisors or experts. They can offer personalized insights, help you optimize your financial strategies, and ensure you make informed decisions.

Mastering personal finance and budgeting is an empowering journey that allows you to take charge of your financial destiny. By implementing these key strategies and financial tips, you can build a strong financial foundation, achieve your goals, and secure a brighter future for yourself and your loved ones.

Remember, financial success is not about perfection; it's about progress and making consistent efforts towards your aspirations. Stay disciplined, stay focused, and stay committed to your financial well-being. As you continue your financial journey, may this guide serve as a valuable companion, guiding you towards a life of financial freedom and fulfillment.

Embarking on Your Financial Journey: Taking Control of Your Money and Future

As you embark on your financial journey armed with the knowledge and insights from "Budgeting: Personal Finance Quick Start Guide," you are taking a significant step towards a brighter and more secure future. Remember, this journey is uniquely yours, and it is a testament to your commitment to taking control of your money and shaping your financial destiny.

Through budgeting, you have learned the art of managing your finances, making conscious spending choices, and setting clear financial goals. You have embraced the power of consistency and adaptability, recognizing that financial success is a dynamic process that requires dedication and openness to change. You have harnessed the strength of celebrating achievements, finding motivation in the progress you make, and building positive financial habits that will serve you well in the long run.

As you continue on this financial path, keep in mind that challenges may arise, and setbacks may occur. However, with the tools and strategies you have acquired, you are equipped to navigate through rough waters and stay on course. Remember to be kind to yourself, practice patience, and view each experience, whether success or setback, as an opportunity to learn and grow.

Your financial journey is not just about reaching a destination but rather a continuous process of improvement and transformation. Embrace the lessons and opportunities that come your way, and remain open to seeking guidance when needed. Whether it's seeking advice from financial experts or learning from others who have achieved financial success, remember that you do not have to walk this path alone.

With every step, you are empowering yourself to take control of your money and your future. By implementing the principles of budgeting, setting clear financial goals, and making informed decisions, you are building a strong foundation that will lead you towards financial freedom and fulfillment.

Congratulations on embarking on this empowering financial journey! Embrace the challenges, cherish the victories, and celebrate the progress you make along the way. As you move forward, never lose sight of the vision you have for your financial future and the life you aspire to create. You have the power to shape your financial destiny, and with each decision you make, you are paving the way for a brighter and more prosperous tomorrow. May this journey be filled with growth, abundance, and the fulfillment of your dreams.

www.ingramcontent.com/pod-product-compliance
Lightning Source LLC
Chambersburg PA
CBHW040321010626
45792CB00024B/2084